Life Is Short— Eat the Donut!

Insights from My Cancer Journey

JANE BIEHL, PHD

ARCHWAY PUBLISHING

Archway Publishing books may be ordered through booksellers or by contacting:

Archway Publishing
1663 Liberty Drive
Bloomington, IN 47403
www.archwaypublishing.com
1 (888) 242-5904

ISBN: 978-1-4808-6395-8 (sc)
ISBN: 978-1-4808-6394-1 (e)

Library of Congress Control Number: 2018948004

Print information available on the last page.

Archway Publishing rev. date: 06/15/2018

DEDICATION PAGE

This book is dedicated to Shruti Trehan M.D. who encouraged me from the beginning to write and publish this book. She is my doctor, my lifesaver, my role model and my friend. She is such an inspiration to all of her patients and I appreciate her immensely!

The Aultman Cancer Center where I go for my treatments recently achieved recognition as one of the top 16 cancer centers in the country from the national Outstanding Achievement Award from American College of Surgeon's Commission on Cancer Accreditation programs. This is a richly deserved award and the fantastic staff from the persons at the front desk, to the laboratory technicians, to the nurses and administration also have supported me on my cancer journey every step of the way. Thank you all! I love my cancer family!!

ACKNOWLEDGEMENTS

I am so fortunate to have many people who have helped me on my cancer journey.

Edlyn and David Theiss have been with me every step of the way. They accompanied me to doctor appointments and drove all over the state to help me get the best medical care possible.

My sister Susan Moellering, and my cousin Miriam Cochran have been there to help me through the bouts of chemo and encourage me all the time.

Many thanks go to Betsy Gorrell, Natalie Jones and Dawn Hayes who helped me with my editing and computer when I did not know what I was doing!

I have the most wonderful neighbors and friends in the world. Thank you Brenda Gibbons, Tod and Betsy Gorrell, Kathy Bernstein, Polly and John Plyter, Ruth Fischer and all the rest of you who bring me food, help me around the house and are always there when needed.

Pastor Dennis Coy and the members of the Congregational United Church of Christ in Canton have been my family throughout this entire time. They help me celebrate the good times, and send prayers and support through the bad times.

The editors and personnel at Cure Today started me on my journey to write and through them I have met many wonderful cancer survivors.

Rudi Hiney, my trainer and friend, and Cathy Cooper, my nutritionist with the Livestrong program at the North Canton YMCA have kept me happy and healthy! Theresa Thorn, my Reiki and polarity therapist keeps me balanced and relaxed!

My fellow cancer survivors who are friends, fellow writers and on committees with me are truly inspirational.

Sita, my hearing ear service dog, has always been by my side and makes me laugh with all of her wonderful zest for life.

And to all of you who have sent up prayers, cards, e-mails and messages on Facebook — you have kept me going! I love you all and you have taught me to cherish every single minute of the day!

CONTENTS

INTRODUCTION

Why I Wrote This Book

"You have Myelodysplastic syndrome. The average life span for this type of cancer is one hundred and four months. You will be on chemo," the doctor told me soberly.

It was April 2010, and my life was about to change forever. I had the "big C" and had just joined a large group of cancer survivors from all over the world. This was not my choice—it was thrust upon me by the mutation of a single cell.

At that time, life was going well. I was working two part-time jobs that I loved and collecting a government pension. One job was as a counselor in a private practice and the other was as an adjunct faculty member at a community college. I had recently moved to a large townhouse. I was still mourning the death of my mother a year ago, but the estate was finally settled. I had a young, healthy hearing ear service dog that I adored, and we worked together, played together, and took walks every night.

I had a loving family, wonderful friends, several hobbies, and an active social life. I exercised regularly and felt good until the anemia hit. Then everything crashed around me, and the pieces of my life were shattered.

This book describes my journey with cancer as a roller-coaster ride. The only way to tell if I am in or out of remission is by undergoing a bone marrow biopsy every six months. After each procedure, I hold my breath to see if I am worse or better.

I have suffered nasty side effects from the chemo; though losing almost all my hearing was the worst of all. I was forced to quit both jobs that I loved. The fatigue has limited many of my social activities. My financial situation deteriorated, and I was forced to move into a much smaller apartment. My dog is now thirteen years old. She has had a surgery because of arthritis and no longer goes on walks. My depression, which I have fought all of my life, hits with a vengeance when I least expect it. That is when the roller coaster goes up; climbing up a steep hill and churning at every turn.

I have become closer to my family. My friends and family have surrounded me with love and support. They have been there with me every step of the way. I have met incredible and inspirational people who were far sicker with lots more on their plates than I ever had. I have begun to figure out what is really important. I am learning not to sweat the small stuff. That is when the roller coaster is going down.

Career wise, I have been fortunate. I was a librarian for nineteen years, a counselor for seventeen years, and an adjunct faculty member for over twenty years. When I was forced to give all this up, I turned to writing. I found a fantastic magazine through my oncologist called *Cure*. I started writing one article, then another, then another. I found the writing therapeutic, and best of all, I was helping others. People with cancer started following me on Facebook. My doctor reminded me that there was very little out there on my type of blood cancer. I finally realized I needed to put the essays together in a book. Cancer survivors need to know they are not alone. Close friends and family told me they never understood the impact of the cancer on me until they read my articles. Much to my surprise, people without this dreaded disease told me how inspirational they found the articles.

I do not know anyone locally with this disease. However, I have met a whole new group of friends through the magazine *Cure*. I have also been contacted by the Aplastic Anemia Myelodysplastic Syndrome International Foundation and have made a slew of contacts there with the help of the wonderful medical editor. I know now there are others like me.

I hope this story about my ups and downs help all of my readers. I also hope you will follow the writing part of my life and contact me. And remember to always eat the donut and *never* give up hope!

INSIGHT I

I Walked in with Anemia and Walked out with Cancer

The moment a patient is told they have cancer, the world stops. The person will remember that moment forever. It is the same sensation as remembering where we were during a terrible time in history such as Pearl Harbor, when President Kennedy was shot, or 9/11.

However, I didn't learn the typical way. Most people find a suspicious lump, have a routine test showing an abnormality, or experience unusual bleeding.

I was tired. That's all—just fatigued. I had anemia once before, which was corrected by a hysterectomy. But this tiredness dragged on and on. The family doctor prescribed the usual iron pills. I took them for a few months and noticed little difference. His office called after I had some blood tests and referred me to an oncologist-hematologist.

For normal people, this would raise a red flag. I was naïve, stupid, in denial, or all three. I still wasn't overly concerned. But let me defend myself a little bit. More than thirty years ago, I had been diagnosed with a rare immune disorder named IgA deficiency. This meant that half of my immune system was gone, but the other half was still working. This type of deficiency cannot be treated by conventional methods like intravenous treatments to build up immunity. It mostly affects the upper respiratory system, causing lots of infections. When an infection started, all the doctors could do was treat me quickly with antibiotics so I didn't get worse. It was not unusual for me to spend weeks at a time on antibiotics. I had periods in between where I would be all right, and then the infections would return. This time, however, the respite periods didn't happen. I was being attacked repeatedly with upper respiratory episodes.

I still was not surprised, because I had several recent stressors, including losing my mother, taking care of the estate, moving to a larger townhouse, and working two demanding part-time jobs.

Never had any doctor informed me, nor had I read research saying, that IgA deficiency was a precursor to a cancer diagnosis. Cancer was the last thing on my mind. My pea brain said, *I have an immune disorder. I am not taking care of myself, and I'm getting multiple infections. So, I have an infection somewhere else in my body they have not found.*

I went to the hematologist, and she took eight vials of blood. I returned a week later, and she explained that all the blood results were fine. I was happy nothing was wrong, but that changed when she said, "Something is causing the anemia, so we have to do a bone marrow biopsy." A sense of alarm crept into my mind. She asked me if I had any questions before we scheduled the biopsy, and I said no. She gave me a very startled look, but I was more worried about the bone marrow procedure than the results. Most reasonable people would be curious by now, but I didn't know what questions to ask.

After the procedure, I returned to the hematologist and asked if she found anything. She told me it was Myelodysplastic syndrome (MDS) and obligingly wrote it down for me. I couldn't pronounce it, much less spell it! She explained that more lab test results needed to be processed to see which type of MDS I had. I had to wait another week.

I went home and perused the Internet. What I read confused me more than helped me. There were five different types of MDS. Some articles called it a cancer, and others stated it was a blood disorder. What did I have?

I found out later that for a long time MDS was considered a rare blood disorder. Recently, however, medical experts concluded that since a single cell had to start the malformation of blood cells, it is classified as a cancer.

I decided on the next visit to bring a friend with me because I was getting overwhelmed. The oncologist explained which type of MDS I had and that the average life span was 104 months. As the room spun around me, I said, "But we found it early." The doctor stated that it was not a typical cancer with stages one through five, but it was treatable by chemotherapy.

I left her office in tears, and my denial stage was over. My friend was a tremendous support as I came to realize what every person diagnosed with cancer has to absorb. I had walked into the doctor's office with anemia and walked out with cancer. I was now one of the many cancer survivors facing a life-changing event. My life was about to change drastically, and I needed to be ready.

INSIGHT 2

The Roller Coaster of MDS

I continued to research this strange-sounding diagnosis. The articles I read revealed the average length of survival ranged from a couple months to nine years, depending on which type of MDS one had. Fortunately, my type of MDS usually allowed someone to live the longest time. The only treatment for this type of cancer was chemotherapy and symptomatic relief. Eventually, I gave up reading about it and decided to face the challenge of living with it.

It took me awhile to recover from the numbness and shock. MDS is a lonely cancer to endure because so few people have it. I can't describe how confused and discombobulated I felt. There are several support groups for breast cancer and other types of cancer, but the numbers of patients is so small for MDS that support groups are difficult to find. The hospital where I was receiving my treatments didn't have navigators for this type of cancer because it is so rare. There was no one available to ask what patients went through until I did additional reading on the Internet. My doctor suggested a magazine called *Cure*. I then discovered this publication was a part of an informative website called Cure Today.

I was originally very naïve. I was placed on a once-a-day oral pill called REVLIMID. Since many people have drastic surgery, radiation, and IV chemo, I figured this oral medication would be a cakewalk.

I was so wrong. Immediately, the fatigue hit me to the point where I was forced to give up one of my part-time jobs. The diarrhea was raging and unpredictable until my oncologist gave me medicine to help. Worst of all, the chemo caused more deafness. I went from being hard of hearing to profoundly deaf. REVLIMID is a derivative of a thalidomide drug, which has the side effect of hearing loss. My oncologist, audiologist, and I didn't know this. The company that produced REVLIMID doesn't warn of this side effect in any of their literature.

I did join a nutrition class for people with cancer and met other people at the cancer center where I received treatments. I soon discovered another unique aspect of MDS. Other patients had certain treatment deadlines such as weeks or months of chemo, and they counted these off until they were finished. Breast cancer survivors across the country have celebratory bells to ring when finished with a round of chemo. I would never have this opportunity because I would be on chemo forever, until it no longer worked. Then my ultimate choices would be a bone marrow transplant, which is risky at my age, or clinical trials.

Honestly, my stomach did a little plunge every time someone asked me when I would be done with chemo, and I explained I never would be finished. I would be on it the rest of my life.

REVLIMID usually only works for two years, but it worked so well for me that I was on it for six years. After it stopped working, I was prescribed VIDAZA. This treatment involved ten shots in the stomach and arms for five days each month. I was forced to stop working even part time because of the fatigue.

I have been on VIDAZA for two years now. The side effects are predictably worse. I get angry, burning welts where the shots are administered and go home to put ice on them for relief. The pain lasts for several days after the treatments. Every time I get angry, I remind myself that I am alive because of VIDAZA.

The only way to know if the cancer is worse or better is to do a bone marrow biopsy. I have had too many to count. I undergo anesthesia, which makes the procedure bearable. However, I am always nervous to receive the results. Sometimes I get good news and other times bad news. I used to love roller-coaster rides as a kid. This feels like being on a roller coaster all the time, and I do not like this ride at all!

Cancer is a lonely disease for every one of us. The doctors can never predict exact side effects because each patient reacts differently. Every cancer patient has his or her own journey and takes that journey alone.

One tremendous hobby I have not yet had to give up is travel. My oncologist is fantastic about timing the treatments, enabling me to take some cruises. She decreases the amount of the chemo so I am not too fatigued to enjoy myself. Cruises are especially nice vacations because I can stay on the ship and sleep if I have to.

I am very fortunate. I have a fantastic oncologist and cancer staff who take great care of me. I have caring and loving family and friends who listen to and support me. They are there in good times and bad. I cherish them more than ever and have learned to be thankful for the gift of every single day.

INSIGHT 3

What Nobody Told Me about Cancer

Cancer. "The big C." Everyone dreads it. All of us have lost loved ones from it, and we know instinctively that after we are diagnosed, life will never be the same. Not only does it affect the cancer survivor, but it also affects the person's friends and family.

It is absolutely true that you will never understand until it happens to you. I have had a compromised immune system my entire life, most likely due to cytomegalovirus. My mother had the flu when she was pregnant with me, and doctors speculate this caused both my immune disorder and severe hearing loss.

Many medical problems had preceded my diagnosis of cancer, including attacks on the kidneys, bladder, and upper respiratory systems. I have been through frequent doctor visits and hospitalizations all of my life. I thought I knew how to navigate the medical system and deal with the insurance companies. I have fought fatigue my entire life due to my compromised immune system, along with the natural fatigue of hearing loss and straining all day to listen and hear.

Despite these medical problems, I had always been able to work both full-time and part-time jobs at the same time. I had even acquired two masters and a doctorate degree.

Therefore, when the diagnosis of Myelodysplastic syndrome at the age of fifty-nine was made, I thought I would be better prepared to be chronically ill than most people. But this diagnosis was very different from the others.

I've had caring and uncaring as well as competent and incompetent doctors in my life. More of them are caring and competent, and I do my best to avoid the ones who are not.

I was unprepared when I sat in the oncologist's office as she tactlessly informed me there was a terminal end to this disease and the average life span for this cancer is 104 months. Her timing for telling me this was awful. I had never had a diagnosis with a final benchmark like this. I clutched my friend's hand and felt the room swim. I realize for cancer survivors this is a long time, but for a person whose parents and grandparents lived into their eighties and nineties, this was devastating. I also couldn't believe as a counselor any doctor would say something so definitive. She needed to be offering hope instead of time limits. She went on to say, "But there may be new drugs." I didn't process that part because I was in shock.

I naïvely thought that all cancers had stages and could be cut out or blasted by chemo and radiation.

I stated, "But we found it early." I didn't understand when she said there were no stages and I would have it for life. She did not explain anything more and left me literally twisting in the wind.

All I wanted at that point was a professional who would fight with me for survival and not just give up with a final road map. I would only be sixty-eight, which is young by today's standards, and I had a lot of living to do! Also, if 104 months was the average life span, that meant half of the people with this disease died sooner than that.

I switched oncologists and found a warm, caring woman who was also very knowledgeable. She assured me that there were options for survival, and she would work with me. She explained that if one option did not work, there were other medicines, clinical trials, and even a bone marrow transplant.

Upon her advice, I went to a university-affiliated hospital where a lot of cutting-edge treatments were being done. I knew I was getting the best care possible, but there are so many things no one ever told me.

I was so anemic that I needed PROCRIT shots for several weeks to increase my red blood cell count. These shots caused me to ache all over as my blood cells started to mutate and change. No one told me that there are people on chemo for life with a blood disorder type of cancer. No one can describe the uncertainty of having a bone marrow biopsy twice a year. It can be an uncomfortable procedure and downright painful without anesthesia. I only allowed that to happen once, but that is not my main concern. The problem with MDS for me is that the numbers of cells that are compromised have ranged from thirty percent to ninety - five percent. Different chemos have lessened the number of cells affected, but my fear is that the number will sometime reach one hundred percent. There is also a chance that the MDS has worsened into leukemia, which is usually fatal when one has MDS first. I went back to the university hospital. The head of the department, who was my doctor, called all over the country and talked to other specialists treating MDS, including the world-famous Mayo Clinic. No doctor understood why these cells were changing so rapidly, nor could they predict the future. They finally decided to continue the chemo and monitor the disease with the biopsies.

REVLIMID had only been on the market for a few years before I started on the regimen, and I was told I would be dead without it. I am grateful beyond belief that I have this medicine, but I am terrified each year of what the future holds.

Yes, doctors and pharmacists and literature all tell you that a side effect is fatigue. For a person who is a high achiever, this was nothing new for me, and I figured I could push through it like I had for fifty-nine years. But this fatigue is not like any other kind. It is malaise. I can be out and about and suddenly get so tired that I need to go to bed immediately. It reminded me of when I had a hysterectomy and would literally fall into bed after only doing a task or two. But this was permanent and a major life adjustment.

At the time of the diagnosis, I worked two part-time jobs, which was the equivalent of one full-time job. After a year of pushing, I finally quit one part-time job and only taught some classes at a community college. After teaching for a couple of hours, I often went home and straight to bed, unable to do anything, including laundry, going out to eat, or even reading or watching TV. As a person who was used to working full time and had pulled all-nighters when working on my dissertation, this was a major change.

I continued to teach and write and volunteer and stay involved. I was told frequently how great I looked in spite of having cancer. But few people, if any, ever understood the price I paid. If I had one busy day, I spent the next day in bed.

The experts and pamphlets I got with the REVLIMID all told me one of the side effects is diarrhea. We all have had that at one time or another. But I was totally unprepared for the raging diarrhea I would endure. It attacked without warning, and I had embarrassing and awful accidents. I was exhausted, humiliated, and often embarrassed, which caused me to stay in bed or near a bathroom for hours on end.

No one warned me that this drug is ototoxic, meaning that it can cause damage to the ear resulting in hearing loss and balance issues. I had heard about ototoxic medications and even taught this in my classes at a local community college. I knew chemo was one of the most toxic drugs for the ears. I casually would say to students that doctors did not think this was serious since "it is better to be deaf than dead."

And then it happened to me. It started with my world and hearing fading away. I would have to ask people to repeat again and again. I no longer could understand anything on TV without captioning, even with my hearing aids on. I was helpless in groups with any noise or going out to noisy restaurants. The world became fainter and fainter.

The professionals did not get it at first. When I saw my audiogram, I told the audiologist that my hearing was worse. She flippantly said, "Well, if it does not change in the next sixty years, you will be okay." She thought it was Presbycusis, which is hearing loss due to aging. I told her this was not fair because I was on chemo. She did another hearing test that showed how significant the loss really was, and then we realized it was the chemo. When I asked my oncologist if the chemo could be causing hearing loss, she answered airily, "Oh, yes, it is an ototoxic medication, and you have a preexisting hearing loss." I was startled as I said I was on a chemo dose of only 5mg. She then explained that this toxic substance builds up in a person's system over time, and I had been on the REVLIMID for four years. After talking to both professionals they realized how this was affecting me and now do hearing tests often to monitor what little hearing remains. The professionals were busy keeping me alive, and they did not realize this was another life-changing blow for me. Fortunately, I knew many people who were hard of hearing and deaf both in the community and at the national level. I knew where to go to receive a captioned telephone and stronger devices to help me with my hearing.

There are so many other events that have been life altering. The huge expenses of being ill have eaten away my savings. The guilt I feel as I look around the waiting room and see people so much sicker than I am bothers me. I have a shoulder that has been reduced to bone grinding on bone, and the orthopedic surgeon wants to do a replacement. He can't because of the danger of my platelet count. I just have to live with the pain. I get tired of acting like I am healthy and being humbled month after month waiting in the oncologist's office for my name to be called and my numbers for blood work to be evaluated. There have been so many bad things about this cancer. But there are wonderful things too.

I found out how much my friends and family care. I was afraid this would turn people away—instead they have flocked around me. I thank God for the special doctors to help me deal with these kinds of emotions day after day. I have a hearing ear service dog that never leaves my side and teaches me to seize each day and take nothing for granted. I have learned that it is okay to sleep in bed all morning and not feel guilty. I no longer waste time on people and things I do not like—life is too short. I am doing the things I can and enjoying every minute.

Yes, I am scared about the future. Yes, I think about it. But every one of us is going to pass away at some point, and once I realized that, it gave me an incredible freedom. The best credo to live by is still the serenity prayer: "God grant me the serenity to accept the things I cannot change; courage to change the things I can; and wisdom to know the difference" (Niebuhr). That wisdom is the hardest of all, but I am getting better with practice!

INSIGHT 4

My Service Dog's Journey with My Cancer

I lead my hearing ear dog, Sita, back to the room where I get the chemo. A staff person greets me as I slip off the orange vest with the forbidding words "Do Not Pet" from my dog's body. Sita follows the person down the hall with tail wagging and heads to the drawer that has the treats. I shut the door to the room where I receive two shots in either the arms or stomach from the chemo nurse. There is a knock on the door, and after opening it, I see my beautiful yellow lab with her gorgeous amber eyes; perky, soft ears; and cold, pink nose eagerly greeting me. I put the vest back on her, and we walk out together. We will follow this routine for four more days this week. I received Sita a year before my mother died. She was trained in the Ohio prison program to be a hearing ear dog. She alerts me by bumping or nudging me with her nose whenever the telephone rings, someone approaches me, or any other unexpected noise. She is my ears, my companion, soul mate, and friend. We have had some struggles along the way. Sita and I visited my mother in assisted living daily right after I brought her home. A year later, Mom died a horrible and painful death with me sobbing at her side and Sita standing next to me. Eighteen months after that, I was diagnosed with cancer. My faithful buddy was with me when I received the devastating news and accompanied me to my follow-up visits to the oncologist. During the six years I was on oral chemo, I visited the doctor monthly. This is where the whole routine started. The staff at the cancer center is all fantastic and loves animals. They brought treats for Sita and told me they looked for my name a couple of days before my visits. They explained that she always makes them feel better. I know they have a rough job, so I was happy to oblige them. They eagerly anticipated her being taken out of her vest, sitting up on her haunches in delight, and chomping happily on her bones. We had discovered Sita had another talent besides being a service dog. The place that trained her agreed with me that she would have been a wonderful therapy dog. She was chosen to be one of the elite, since only one of one hundred dogs makes it to the finish line as a service dog. Her sweet and laid-back disposition plus her soft-looking face charms people who are ill. The staff soon began taking her in to see the patients receiving chemo, and the smile on their faces filled the room. She knew how to be a therapy dog during those moments. But as soon as the vest went back on, she changed. Sita walked out and strutted with me down the hallway, ready to be working again.

To my alarm, soon after I was diagnosed with the cancer, Sita began snapping at other dogs when they approached me. It happened several times, and I was hysterical because this one vice could end her career

9

as a service dog. I was driving my car with a friend who was a certified dog trainer in the passenger seat. I began to cry as I told her what was going on with Sita. As I told my story, Sita, who had been lying down in the back seat, reached her face over the front and nudged me to comfort me. "There it is," explained my friend. "You are anxious and upset after your mother's death and the cancer diagnosis. She is picking up on all your emotions and trying to protect you the only way she knows how. If you calm down, she will." The light bulb illuminated in my head. I was so stressed out with the changes in my life that I had almost ruined my dog. Besides, I was learning that being so worried made my health worse. I began to settle down and so did she. When my chemo was switched to shots in the stomach, I feared she would become upset with this new type of treatment. I implored the staff to help me, and they did. They gave her treats and petted her while I was getting the needles, and the other patients loved her!

As I think back over the ten years that I have been partnered with this beautiful creature, I reflect on how fortunate I was to have a dog that loved me unconditionally. I was also fortunate to have a fantastic oncologist and staff that understood and helped me and receive a chemo that allows me to live a long life with my companion. I am truly blessed!

INSIGHT 5

My Love/Hate Relationship with Chemo

I compare my love/hate relationship with chemo to how I felt when I got my first hearing aid at age six. I had to wear this ugly, awkward, square box on my chest with a cord going into my ear. My mother made a little cloth cushion, and the aid was attached to my underwear or my bra every minute I was at school. The hearing aid caused me embarrassment, ridicule, and bullying all through school.

But I also loved this boxy little device. I could actually hear words and distinguish sounds when I put it on. It allowed me to be more "normal."

I feel the exact same way about my chemo. I hate the week every month that I have it. For five days in a row, I roll out of bed and drive to the other side of the county to the hospital where the cancer center is. For five days, I sit in the waiting room with all the other poor patients waiting to be called for my chemo. I trot after the nurse, and when I reach the infusion room, I get two large, painful shots in the stomach. I decided after several months not to get the shots in the arm anymore because it hurt less when I get them in the large area of the stomach.

Afterward, I eat out for lunch and take home something for dinner. I come home and nap. The shots make me very sore, so I lie in my bed with ice packs. I rarely go out for dinner. The chemo zaps my energy, and I keep a low profile for the week. I may do some light chores, some reading, and some writing and be on my computer. Sometimes I just feel like lying on my recliner and watching TV. Even grocery shopping is problematic because carrying bags hurts my stomach. I finally succumbed and got a handicapped sticker to help me during these times.

Of course, all cancer survivors are familiar with the side effects of nausea, diarrhea, and constipation. Fortunately, I have learned to take the medicine the doctor prescribes right away to keep the symptoms from manifesting. I hate these weeks and dread the treatments. I center my life on the chemo and planning not to be busy.

However, here is where it gets complex. I have learned not to love—but to respect—the chemo. It is keeping me alive a little bit longer. It allows me to function the other three weeks of the month. It is the dreaded chemo that is saving me. Just like the hearing aids I wear, which are now smaller and hidden behind the ears, enable me to hear.

I have discovered something else. It is not so bad to have a week off. I am an overachiever and feel guilty for lying around. But sometimes it is good for me to nap when I feel like it, to daydream a little bit, to lounge around and watch television. I do not have to be productive every single moment to be a worthwhile person. It is during these quiet moments that ideas come to me for writing articles, solving problems, and I pray with a wonderful God.

I seldom wear my hearing aids around the house. After going out socially and straining so hard to understand conversation, I come home exhausted. I use my captioned TV, captioned telephone, and computer for listening and communicating. For some people, this silence would be overwhelming, but for me it is therapeutic.

Also, that very same hearing loss I experienced as a child has introduced me to a whole group of deaf and hard-of-hearing friends. I have learned sign language and even taught a class called Deaf Culture at a community college for several years. So the loss became a huge benefit in my life.

There is still another wonderful advantage to chemo week. I truly believe the nurses, technicians, receptionists, doctors, and staff who works in any cancer center is special. What a privilege to be surrounded by them! During this week, I get to see them every day. I know their personalities, ask about their families, and friend them on Facebook. To me, they are angels on earth.

I even have made friends on Facebook with other patients I met in the waiting room. And every one of these patients has their own unique journey as cancer survivors. I am on a patient advisory committee for the cancer center. And now I am writing articles for the website Cure Today and meeting other survivors who help and inspire me.

So, yes, I have a love/hate relationship with both my hearing aids and my chemo. But I treasure the fact that the hearing aids allow me to hear well. Most important of all, the chemo is keeping me alive!

INSIGHT 6

Parceling My Energy with Cancer

"You look great. You have so much energy. You must be feeling good." I am bombarded with comments like this from well-meaning friends and relatives daily. Sometimes I just want to scream, "It is all an act, a façade. I am exhausted, and all I want to do is go home and sleep." It is *not* just being tired…

I have three graduate degrees and pulled my share of all-nighters. Chemo fatigue is different. No amount of sleep will bring back the energy like it did when I was worn out from working or studying. There are times when I get out of bed feeling like a bucket of lead is weighing me down.

Most people would be surprised to hear me say that the worst side effect, besides the hearing loss, is fatigue. I am very social and always on the go.

However, I am learning to parcel my energy. What does this mean? The definition of parcel is "the act of separating or dividing into parts and distributing, allotting, or apportioning." I know now that I need to allot a certain amount of energy to each task I do. Especially during chemo week, I can only perform one major task each day. All of my energy goes into that activity, whether it is meeting with friends for dinner, conducting an educational program with my hearing ear service dog, or working at home on bills and correspondence. I give all I have to that task, and then I head for bed and collapse.

The tricky part about parceling energy is that this process is different for each person. Some people are working and need to continue to pay their insurance or medical bills. Others have spouses, children, and grandchildren they want to spend time with. Still others feel that their volunteer work is important. And some people want to travel.

We each deal with this a different way. I added an extra career to my résumé, which is writer. This career can be done on my own timeline. If I feel a little more energy, I write; if not, I don't. I take cruises for vacations, so I can rest in between stops at tourist points. For my volunteer work, instead of showing up weekly at an agency, I send cards to persons in my church and can do that on my better days. I also do programs with my service dog, and that is the only event for the day.

Now I no longer feel like a fraud when I am told I look wonderful. I have no desire to explain to people I really feel lousy and want to go home to bed. I smile and say, "Yes, I feel good today."

All cancer survivors need to find their own path to kicking cancer's butt. It is truly a process. We do not have to give up and do nothing. But we do have to concentrate on what is most important to us. My energy is mostly gone, but I pace it to do the activities that are the most meaningful to me. I have a friend who is paralyzed from the waist down and can no longer teach classes and do the volunteer work she used to do for her church. She learned to knit blankets while in her bed and wheelchair for people who needed them. She is a fantastic person and such an inspiration to me. Even if we are bedridden, there is something we can do.

The best part is I am learning what is most important in my life, which is spending time with much-loved friends and family! No matter what else is going on in my life, I find time for that, and you will too.

INSIGHT 7

Is Your Chemo Causing Hearing Loss?

The world is getting fainter and fainter. You are missing conversations you heard before. You can no longer distinguish the words to a song on the radio. You ignore it all because you are a cancer survivor and have more important things on your mind like chemo, radiation, doctor appointments, and just surviving. What you may not realize is that it is all related.

Many successful chemo drugs are ototoxic, which literally means "poisoning of the ears." Some drugs destroy the tiny hairs in the cochlea that transmit sound. Other drugs attack structures of the ear such as the cochlea or block sounds to the auditory nerve.

These drugs can also cause tinnitus, which means a ringing or other noise in the ear when no sound is present. Other side effects, such as dizziness and balance problems, also can occur from these ototoxic medications (Bauman 2010).

As a consumer, you need to be aware that new drugs are not routinely tested for toxicity. The available information only results after reports have been filed with the manufacturer of the drug. At that point, the manufacturer must report side effects to the Food and Drug Administration (Hammond 2013).

One chemo drug that is commonly known to be poisonous to the ears is Cisplatin. Many chemo patients have a compromised immune system and use other common medications known to be dangerous, such as the "mycin" family, including Neomycin, Tobramycin, Erythromycin, and Vancomycin. Nonsteroidal anti-inflammatory drugs (NSAIDS) such as ibuprofen and naproxen can also damage the ears, although if they are discontinued, the effects are usually reversible (Kaufman 2000).

Loop diuretics may be problematic too, causing damage to the auditory nerve. And the well-known drug aspirin, when consumed in large amounts, may be harmful (Rosen 2014).

Noise pollution presently is one of the leading causes of hearing loss in the country. The National Institute on Deafness and Other Communication Disorders (2015) estimates 14 percent of Americans between ages twenty and sixty-nine, or twenty-six million Americans, have hearing loss due to noise pollution. Therefore, if a cancer patient is on an ototoxic drug *and* is being exposed to noise pollution, the chances of losing his or her hearing increase significantly.

To add even more confusion to this problem, the drug is frequently listed under the trade name and not the generic name (Suss 1993). Both need to be thoroughly researched.

This is exactly what happened to me. I was on the oral drug REVLIMID. There were no side effects listed for hearing loss, but I was on this chemo for six years when most patients are only on it for two. My hearing loss dropped to the profound range. I discovered that REVLIMID is a derivative of thalidomide, which is known to be ototoxic and listed as such. My cancer worsened, and presently I am on VIDAZA, which is known to cause hearing loss.

I am extremely fortunate because my audiologist and oncologist work well together. I am desperately attempting to hang on to the little hearing I have left. Every couple of months, I receive an audiogram that is sent to my oncologist. Sometimes a patient can be taken off an ototoxic drug, but not with chemo, which is life-saving.

The expert on ototoxic medications is Neil Bauman. His well-known book is titled *Ototoxic Drugs Exposed: The Shocking Truth about Prescription Drugs, Medications, Chemicals and Herbals That Can (and Do) Damage Our Ears* can be checked out online or at the library. He has discovered over 743 drugs known to be ototoxic, and this number continues to expand.

In summary, be informed and develop a team with your hearing expert and oncologist. Do your research carefully. If you can be taken off a dangerous drug, be sure to celebrate. If not—well, it is better to be deaf than dead, but I would rather not be either one!

INSIGHT 8

The Guilt of Outliving Friends—and Cancer

I was in hospice with a very dear friend, saying goodbye and waiting for the breathing tube to be removed. Sharry was such a wonderful person, and we adored her. The last request my friend made was that she wished she could have a dog with her. Her whole life was centered on animals: grooming them, taking care of them, and rescuing them. Her daughter had texted me that Sharry was in hospice. I asked her if she wanted Sita, my beautiful service dog, to come. Her daughter replied that she needed Sita and told her mother that Sita was on her way. Sharry nodded before she slipped into the coma. Both of us are certain Sharry understood she would have a canine with her when she passed. Since Sita was a service dog, she was allowed in the room, and she immediately became a therapy dog. She climbed up on the bed next to Sharry and refused to leave her. Sharry was surrounded by a circle of friends and family crying softly because we loved her so much.

A pang entered my heart when Sharry's mother asked me how I was doing with my cancer. Sharry worried constantly about me and took care of Sita when I was away. She was there with my dog when I took my mother to the emergency room. Now she was the one dying instead of me. I replied shakily, "I am fine, and I am alive." I felt so guilty. I still miss Sharry terribly, and it has been several years. That same year, I lost two other close friends to cancer—one of them was Sharry's husband. I lost another dear friend to a heart attack. All of them were younger than me. Since then, I have lost more friends to this devastating cancer disease. Just a couple of month ago, I spoke at a celebration-of-life service for a member of my church who passed from cancer. My voice trembled the entire time I spoke. Ironically, we shared the same oncologist and saw each other in the waiting room frequently, but her vicious cancer took her in a very short time. I miss her every Sunday and know she was a far better person than I am. Hell yes, I feel guilty! I am single and these people had spouses and children and grandchildren to miss them. Why am I still alive eight years later? Why does a loving God, or higher power, or whatever we believe in, allow one person to die and another to survive? I truly do not believe that higher power is picking out one person who deserves to live and someone else to die. That is not my concept of a loving spirit, and my faith in God helps me through all the terrible times.

I feel that life can be random and unfortunate. Drunk drivers may kill one person while another survives. Horrible storms may devastate one family and the neighbors are all right. With cancer, so many factors enter the equation of survival: What type (mine is a slower-moving one), when was it discovered, what type of medical help is available, and is the environment causing some problems? An example would be someone living next to a chemical factory. Why do we get the disease in the first place? Sometimes it boils down to one tiny cell that starts the whole terrible process. I could go on and on. The reality is that we all die sometime. How do I cope with survivor's guilt? Not always well—I always have and will feel guilty. I do think one of the most insensitive things to ever say is that God still wanted me alive for something. That is such a conceited and awful approach and sounds like other people do not deserve to be alive. Every one of us has unfinished business and a reason to live, even an elderly person with a pet. But what I can say is that during my time left on earth, I will support the families left behind to grieve their loved ones. A card, an email, a text or a phone call can make all the difference in the world to the friends and family. Also, I can take advantage of every single moment I have left. To feel guilty helps no one, but to reach out helps someone. I concentrate on reaching out.

INSIGHT 9

The Wonder of the Oncology Nurse

One of the most underrated professions in the world is nursing. The doctors are definitely at the top of the medical pyramid, but any smart doctor will acknowledge that they couldn't administer care or cure their patients without the nurses.

It is the nurses who are in the hospital in the middle of the night when a crisis occurs and a decision must be made to contact the doctor. It is the nurses whose sharp eyes observe any subtle change that could be life-threatening and alert the doctors. It is the nurses who administer the medications and watch for adverse reactions. It is the nurses who hold the patients' hands through pain, vomiting, side effects, and sometimes passing over to the other side.

I am not a nurse myself, but I know and respect them. I had several nursing students in classes when I taught at a community college. I watched them study terminology I could never pronounce, much less understand.

I have been the recipient of nursing care in several settings ranging from surgery, to office, to oncology. I have several friends and a relative who work to the brink of exhaustion daily, but truly know what they are doing is lifesaving.

However, the oncology nurses are the ones I know the best. There is no other specialty like this one. These are the people who, along with my oncologist, have not only kept me alive, but motivated me to undergo painful chemo.

While I was on oral chemo for six years, I passed the chemo nurses in the hallway when visiting my doctor and observed how nice they were. When my cancer worsened, I needed them to administer my shots for five days each month. I was terrified and experienced nightmares about the bad reactions I would have. I stewed for days and felt close to tears when I met my first chemo nurse for treatments, along with one of the special lab technicians.

These two people were fantastic! They gave me a brochure and explained all the side effects. They explained why the shots had to be taken in the stomach and the back of the arms. They used just the right combination of empathy and humor to relax me.

I also have a rare immune disorder and experienced several problems during the first cycle. At one point, I asked the nurses to "let me go and die." Of course, I didn't mean it, but I was so sick I didn't care. The alternating diarrhea, constipation, pain, fatigue, chills, and fever all overwhelmed me. My stomach looked sunburned and began to peel. (It still does, but I ignore it now.) It was not my finest hour.

To add to the nightmare, my doctor's father died suddenly, and she was out of the country. However, the nurses soldiered on, emailed her and kept me on track—each and every one of them!

I lived through that cycle, and the next, and the next. While the pain never goes away, I do know what to expect. My doctor returned, and I felt like my mother was back!

I asked one of the nurses how they do this job, because they lose so many of their patients. Her answer thrilled me. "I have been here eighteen years and taken care of the same patients for eighteen years. I also get to meet nice people like you. What is there not to like?" Wow! What a terrific attitude. Another nurse confided to me that they get to know their patients so well that when we are walking down the hall, they can tell how we feel and may alert the doctors. I also have a service dog, and the nurses are wonderful to her also. Since my service dog is an extension of me, that is very important.

Oncology nurses are with us day in and day out. We know they are fighting every battle with us. The other cancer patients and I have told them repeatedly that they are family. One of the nurses mentioned to me that they see us more than their own family, and that is true.

So what makes oncology nurses so special? They take on a profession where they know they will lose their patients. They do everything they can to fight and prolong the patients' lives. They administer medications that give people better quality of life. They know all about me and my family, my hobbies, and my vacations. They are always there to laugh with, comfort me, and hold my hand. No wonder these people are so special. I call them my "angels on earth."

INSIGHT 10

The Making of an Oncologist

Before I had cancer, I wondered why anyone would want to be an oncologist. My thoughts were you took care of all these really sick people who were bedridden with tubes running everywhere. You lost more patients than any other doctor. So why would anyone choose this specialty? I was naïve and very wrong.

I think I have the most fantastic oncologist in the world. She is caring, compassionate, and knowledgeable. All her patients love her. My family doctor of twenty-five years has commented to me, "You will never find anyone who cares for you more than she does," and he is correct.

But I have noticed something else. My friends who have other oncologists often feel the same way about their specialist. What makes the oncologist so unique?

Other doctors come and go in our lives. Maybe you see a primary care physician once a year. Increasingly, nurse practitioners are the ones who take care of us. Presently, we don't even see our family doctors in the hospital, because they have hospitalists for that. A surgeon takes care of a surgery and their job is done, unless one is unfortunate enough to need them again. Some people with chronic illnesses may see their endocrinologist or gastroenterologist frequently.

But the oncologist is different. It is the oncologist who often has to break the news to the patient that the diagnosis is cancer, which scares every one of us. He or she has to determine the treatment and decide how much or little chemo to give. Then this doctor is forced to watch patients become fatigued, suffer terrible side effects, lose their hair, and change their lives forever. Meanwhile, the oncologist needs to be the cheerleader when a patient wants to give up on a potentially lifesaving treatment.

Unless specializing in just one type of cancer, most oncologists are expected to be on top of new treatments for every type of cancer. They confer with other oncologists and family physicians to determine what is best for each patient. They also perform difficult bone marrow biopsies and give the depressing or sometimes happy results. They reassure family members who are angry because more cannot be done.

Ultimately it is the oncologist, along with the nurses, who may be holding a patient's hand as he or she is in palliative care or hospice and transitioning over to the other side.

In summary, the life of an oncologist is an emotional roller coaster. Why would anyone want to do this?

The answer has come to me after spending eight years in a cancer center having chemo. I talk to other patients who have told me their doctors have kept them alive for ten years, twelve years, and even longer with good quality of life. My own oncologist knows my personality, my flaws, and my talents. Indeed, it was she who encouraged me to write about my experiences, which has been so cathartic.

I can only imagine her fantastic feelings as she tells some of her patients that they are cancer free and can go out to resume their lives. They will always remember the person who saved their lives. If something changes, she will be there as a safety net with her calm demeanor to help them through. Others she gives many extra months or years of quality life they would not have otherwise. Some she has prepared for the difficult journey to dying and beyond, and she does that with the utmost compassion. And there are patients like me who presently have a wonderful life. However, I will be on chemo until I pass. I know she will be there when it stops working—because she cares.

As a former counselor, I know research has shown that there is not one type of therapy that is more beneficial than another. The only determining factor to a successful therapy is the relationship between the therapist and the client. I always viewed my job as a spiritual journey between me and my client. I'm talking about that connection in the universe that is so important in any relationship, but especially a healing one.

My oncologist tells me she feels the same way. I asked her once how she does such a difficult job. She answered that her higher power gave her the spiritual strength to treat her patients. What an incredible journey for her!

Yes, I am alive today because of the miracles of research and modern medicine. Many of us are. But we are also alive because of the spiritual healing and connection between doctor and patient. That is why a doctor becomes an oncologist and why the making of an oncologist is so special. Bless all of them!

INSIGHT II

Being Vulnerable with Cancer Is Okay

When a person is initially diagnosed with a blood cancer such as Myelodysplastic syndrome, it feels like a life sentence. The oncologist informs you that you will never be off the chemo. Every time you enter the cancer center, you know there is no end and you will be doing this for the rest of your life.

But how does one handle the whole ordeal? How do you balance the doctor visits, the biopsies, the side effects, and the constant fatigue that never goes away? Your life changes drastically when you realize you will never feel as good as you did before your cancer.

I had decided from the get-go that I was not going to complain. I was going to be an example of being positive, happy, and thankful to be alive, which I am. But I needed to learn to be vulnerable. What a lesson it has been for me.

After a particularly tough time of having intestinal flu, hurting from the horrible chemo shots, battling the grayness of Ohio winter, and sleeping many hours away, I decided to reach out. I am fortunate to have many friends all over the world who I keep in touch with on Facebook. After much deliberation, I wrote what was really in my heart. I explained that I was tired, sad, and discouraged. I emphasized that I did not want to be a whiner and felt fortunate to be alive. I acknowledged that there were people much worse off than I am.

Still, I asked for support and prayers to help me through this terrible time

The response brought me to tears. Within hours I had comments from people in Japan, Holland, and all over the United States. I heard from friends and neighbors nearby who I seldom see. I got messages from students at the community college where I used to teach. Overwhelmingly, people told me that I was not a whiner. They thanked me for asking for help. They assured me that I was in their thoughts and prayers. A couple of people thanked me for breaking the facade and "being real!"

People reassured me that I was strong and would get through this. They offered to come and help me with food, cleaning, and even walking my service dog when I was too tired.

The very post that I was afraid to write because I would appear weak and babyish had the opposite effect. People responded with support and love and told me that I was being strong by asking for help.

It is okay to be upset and depressed. It is all right to be vulnerable and ask for help when you need it. Most people want to help the cancer survivor, but we need to tell them how.

So, if things are not going well, if you feel terrible, if you need someone to talk to or walk the dog, tell your friends and family. If you are religious, ask for prayers. Most people in this world do want to help and they do care. You have to let them know what you need and let them assist you. They know you would do the same for them.

INSIGHT 12

Worry About or Embrace Cancer: It's My Choice

One of the hardest parts of having this disease is waiting for the results of the two bone marrow biopsies I get each year to test how many of my cells are mutated. It takes several weeks to get the complete report back.

The only way to diagnose and treat this disease is with the bone marrow biopsy, or chromosome/cytogenetic testing. What the doctor (and I) is looking for is the number of abnormal 5q minus gene. The number of abnormal cells has fluctuated between 30 to 95 percent since my diagnosis. My oncologist is trying to keep the MDS from evolving into leukemia. While many kinds of leukemia are treatable, the prognosis for someone who had MDS first is usually fatal. We hope with each procedure that the percentage is stable or better. With each procedure, I hold my breath wondering what the cells will tell me this time. I know I am approaching that 104-month benchmark. The chance of living past ten years is not great. However, I was younger than most people when diagnosed.

I would be lying if I did not admit that I get extremely depressed at times. I wonder when we are planning family events if I will be here for milestones. I am hoping to make it to my seventieth birthday and have a huge party!

I never knew how anyone could go through something like this and survive. The human spirit is amazing, and we do rise to the occasion. My faith has become stronger, and I find my church to be a huge support for me. My family and friends mean more to me than ever before.

All of this has been wonderful, but the most helpful activity is my own self-talk. I have a doctorate in counseling. I used to instruct my clients to think positive instead of negative thoughts. It is absolutely a fact that the brain is not able to harbor two thoughts at once. It may be separated by only a millisecond, but the brain cannot think something positive and negative at the same time. This is the theory behind the popular counseling technique cognitive therapy.

So what I do is this. When I get scared, when my medical reports are bad, when I am really hurting from the chemo, or wondering how long I have to live, I remind myself that I just spent fifteen minutes or more worrying about negative events. Because the cancer and my chemo drain me, I do not have much energy now. Do I *really* want to waste my remaining energy on being upset, or do I want to embrace adventure? These fifteen minutes of stewing accomplished nothing except rob me of my zest for life. If I had spent fifteen minutes enjoying the sunset, talking with friends, or writing an article, I would be much happier. Of course, I have my days of feeling sorry for myself, and that is okay too. Mentally I need to have some time to vent. But I dare not let this attitude consume me, or I will spiral down the drain and never come back up.

This type of self-talk takes practice, and replacing negative thoughts with positive ones is not easy. Therapists work very hard with their patients to teach them to do this. One of the biggest revelations I discovered as a counselor was that my clients would berate themselves by the hour—even children. They would tell me over and over again how bad they were and all the things that they did wrong.

I would stop them and tell them that before they left my office, they had to tell me five good things about themselves. And most of them could not do it! I would guide them by saying, "You were very polite," "You did something kind for a neighbor," or "You look very nice today." It becomes a habit to talk oneself into being positive instead of negative.

It is extremely important for cancer survivors to be positive. They have so little energy that they cannot embrace worrying. They must embrace happy thoughts, or the results can be, well, fatal.

Actually seizing the day is good advice for anyone, regardless of whether they have cancer. I cannot choose what happens to me in life. I can only choose how I react. Am I going to worry or be positive and enjoy life? It is up to me!

INSIGHT 13

Chemo Fog Is Real—and Scary!

I am sixty-seven years old, so now I am considered "elderly." It was really a shock the first time a student called me that!

For years before that benchmark, I had joked about becoming old. I would laugh about forgetting things unless I wrote them down. However, behind my comments was an edge, because my father had Alzheimer's and died from choking. My biggest fear is that I will develop that disease.

This may be the reason I hate the chemo fog so much. One of the most embarrassing moments of my life was when I was at a local bank and couldn't remember my phone number! I remedied that by putting my own number in my cell phone. I apologized profusely to the bank employee, and he was very gracious about it. I still am not sure he believed me when I blamed chemo fog. Most people do not understand this problem.

I taught college classes for seven years after being diagnosed with cancer. We all know chemo is cumulative, and the fog only gets worse with time. I remember the last couple of years when I was lecturing, I sometimes had to search for certain well-known words in a lecture I knew by heart. A scary little infinitesimal pause would happen until I found the word. I'm not sure the students ever noticed it, but I did. I wondered how long I would be able to continue teaching. This cut me to the core, since I was passionate about my students. Eventually, my cancer worsened, and I was forced to resign for physical reasons. I was honestly relieved that decision was made by my doctor.

Only another person with chemo fog can understand the panic when searching for a certain word or phrase. My friends and family often see me struggle and supply the missing words for me. Before chemo fog, I would sometimes forget a word or phrase but remember the phrase later. Now I do not retain the word or phrase at all.

I have a PhD in counseling and have carefully studied the brain. The short-term memory is usually the part affected by dementia or head trauma. If one talks to a person with dementia, they may remember events from a long time ago, but not whether they had breakfast that day. Much publicity has been generated on concussions and the damage to the brain in sports. Presently, the American Cancer Society is doing some research on "chemo brain," as they call it. Doctors are exploring ways to protect the brain from the side effects of chemo. This is positive news for cancer survivors!

To compound my problem, I will be on chemo the rest of my life, however long that is. The chemo has accumulated in my system for seven long years. However, people who have stopped chemo tell me remnants of chemo fog remain years later, and I believe them.

Another fact that complicates everything for me is that I am now profoundly deaf from the chemo. This results in many errors in communication. I don't hear people calling me. Recently a TSA official screamed at me at the airport for not stopping when she yelled at me. I held up a line at Starbucks because I thought the barista kept asking me if I wanted "wimp" coffee (my interpretation) instead of "whip." I frequently respond with wrong answers or ignore people because I don't hear them. So now many people think I am either snooty or stupid—take your pick.

It is impossible to explain to people about chemo fog. I have had well-meaning friends make fun of me "losing my mind."

So now I have two choices. I can spend a lot of time explaining to people that I am suffering from cancer treatments and deafness, or I can just say nothing. All of us face this challenge sooner or later.

What is the solution? I usually try to tell family and close friends what is really happening. I find most acquaintances are too busy or self-involved to care, and unless they are really digging, I say nothing.

I am eternally grateful for informational sites like Cure Today, the American Cancer Society, the National Cancer Institute, American Association for Cancer Research, the Aplastic Anemia and MDS International Foundation, and other popular websites that share information on chemo fog or chemo brain. Many evenings I get on my computer and read articles from people who are going through what I am, and I'm grateful to them for sharing.

Finally, I keep my sense of humor and perspective. Some of this is rather funny, and the rest of it I cope with by asking myself one question: Is it really important in the scheme of things what people think of me? After all, I am a cancer survivor, and I am alive!

INSIGHT 14

Living Naturally

One of the benefits of a cancer diagnosis for me was a complete lifestyle change. I was fortunate to have several friends and family to help me along the way.

Sometimes patients with cancer go into remission, but other times they don't. Even patients in remission need an extra boost to their immune system. Every cancer survivor is on their own unique journey, but one fact is true for all of us—it is important to have the immune system be as strong as possible.

When I write about "natural," I am not talking about going off to Mexico or another foreign country for alternative medicine. I am talking about helping the immune system by relieving stress and becoming stronger to fight those lousy cells.

It truly seemed that the opportunities to do this dropped in my lap. I had belonged to my local YMCA for fifteen years. Unknown to me, they had an exercise program called Livestrong. Athletic trainers across the country are specifically trained to assist cancer survivors either undergoing chemo or finished with treatment. Participants work on a modified exercise program. People meet as a group several times a week with the trainer. I chose to pay for an individual trainer because it was so much easier for me to hear. Unknown to me, all chemo causes balance problems, and I wondered why I was falling so easily. Many local YMCAs are a part of the Livestrong program.

Our YMCA has additional services for cancer survivors. The cancer center where I go assists with the cost. A licensed dietician comes in several times a week and teaches cancer survivors how to eat better when feeling nauseated, having diarrhea, or they need to lose or gain weight. She is so knowledgeable, and I love her classes! We even visit a local grocery store monthly to sample healthy products and see what we like. Another licensed dietician is there from the store to help us.

I personally was experiencing severe diarrhea from the chemo, and over-the-counter medications were not working. The dietician recommended Kefir, a type of yogurt, and it helped more than anything else. I still eat it every day with some healthy flaxseed on top. Kefir has the probiotics we need to strengthen our immune system. My trainer and dietician work closely together and have helped a great number of people throughout the years.

Another friend contacted me about using essential oils and aromatherapy. I was surprised when she shared with me that one of the best cancer centers in the country, MD Anderson Cancer Center, is using these as a part of their program. I am now working with an experienced distributor on the correct oils to help me personally with the side effects of chemo. One caution: be sure you work with a reputable distributor rather than buying cheaper ones over the counter because some of these oils have been watered down and are not as effective.

There are several excellent books that are free online to give you information on the oils. For example, I have a diffuser, and there is no doubt in my mind that the lavender and orange oils not only make my bedroom smell better but help me to relax and sleep more soundly.

The hospital where I go for treatments also sponsors Reiki classes. I go to a special friend who does Reiki. I have used her wonderful services for several years and am so relaxed when I leave, I feel limp! This is definitely a boost to my immune system and a stress reducer. Yoga is also supposed to be a big help, but I have yet to try that!

Another wonderful natural product made a huge difference for me. I receive shots in the stomach, and I experience severe burning and reddened skin at the injection sites for a couple of weeks afterward. The blisters are quite painful, and OTC remedies do not help. My cousin found a store where all their cream products are made from natural oils and exotic butters. She bought some samples for me to try. The store owners make every one of their products by hand. The difference between these creams and the OTC creams was night and day. I later visited the store myself, and they said several of their customers are patients recovering from chemo and radiation. You can check the Internet for a distributor near you or one that does mailing to your home.

I am not claiming that diet, exercise, essential oils, Reiki, handmade creams, and other natural products will cure your cancer, but they can boost your immune system and make you feel good. And we all want that whether we have cancer or not!

INSIGHT 15

Coping with Cancer-Related Fatigue

It is early afternoon, and I am enjoying lunch with my friends. We are laughing, talking, and having a great time.

Without warning, their voices begin to fade, and I can no longer concentrate. I excuse myself politely, pay my check, and drive home. I immediately fall into bed and sleep for the next couple of hours. Frustrating as this was, I needed to do that before I could finish my chores for the rest of the day.

I slept in this morning and feel good. I take my service dog and do grocery shopping and run errands. When we return home, she is by the door ready for her daily walk. I collapse between the sheets to sleep before I have enough energy to take her.

I have paid a handsome price to see a real live theater play I love. I am relaxed and listening to the music. Suddenly my eyes close, and I am struggling to stay awake.

Welcome to the world of real fatigue. The combination of cancer and chemo makes me chronically, unremittingly, and forever tired. When I mention this as a side effect, only people with cancer and other chronic conditions really get it.

I am on constant chemo and will be forever, but even people who have stopped chemo tell me they still are tired for years afterward. This makes sense if you realize that chemo is pouring poison into your system to destroy the bad cells, but it is also attacking the good ones. Resulting fatigue is unavoidable. Another name for this type of tiredness is malaise. I think most of us have figured out our chemo cycles and have an idea how long it will take to get at least some of our energy back before the next round.

In my experience, it does no good to try and explain the amount of fatigue cancer survivors go through. I put in all-nighters in college, many long days and nights working two jobs, stayed up countless nights writing a dissertation, and have been in the emergency room until the wee hours of the morning with relatives. The big difference was this—one night's sleep and I felt better. With chemo, fatigue is a tiredness that never goes away.

So how do I cope? If I mention to someone that I am tired from the chemo, and they say, "Oh yes, I am getting older, and I know what you mean," I just smile and nod. I honestly feel guilty about the fatigue and that I have to take naps. That old voice instilled by my parents about never being idle still echoes in my head.

The only way I can handle this is self-talk. I need to remind myself that sleeping this much is not laziness but part of the healing process. I can beat myself up, but then I realize I am still alive! I am exhausted, but I do the best I can. If that means more naps, so be it.

I have been forced to realize that I can no longer work an eight-hour day and then come home and do a bunch of stuff around the house. I may putter around or go out and get groceries or be with friends. I may function for four hours or two hours or one hour or none. But I am enjoying another wonderful day. Hey, I never said it was easy. I still feel guilty after seven years for "slacking off." I also have learned a great deal.

It is fun to go out on my patio and have a cup of coffee whenever I feel like it. My dog loves her belly rubs. My cat enjoys my lap. There are lots of good books to read. If I want to spend lazy times on Facebook, that is okay. Yes, I have seen that episode of *Law and Order* before, but I like that show. And my friends enjoy my staying and talking over lunch or dinner, instead of hurrying home to grade papers like I did when I was teaching. The sunsets I get to watch are beautiful.

Yes, I am constantly tired. Yes, I want to do more. But there is much more to life than working all the time. Naps and lying around aren't so bad either. I am happy to be here on earth for a little while longer.

Sorry—I am tired now and have to go take a nap!

INSIGHT 16

Cancer Survivors, Don't Burn the Midnight Oil

One of the hardest things about having cancer and the resulting treatments is the constant fatigue. Most of us lead busy lives and are totally unprepared when the tiredness hits us like a ton of bricks.

The problem is learning to sort out what needs to be done now and what can wait. Priorities have to be set. We all know that everything seems important when you are too weak to do anything! We ask ourselves what can possibly be postponed until tomorrow.

I know personally when I worked and went to school and kept an insane schedule, I would go and go and go until I was running on empty. I always felt there was a little more oil in the lamp, until I got sick. My family doctor would tell me to take it easy, which I did for a day or two. Soon I was back up and running again.

Cancer isn't like that. The fatigue lasts longer. The chemo and radiation treatments do not make one fatigued for only a day or two—it can last for months. With my type of cancer, I will be on chemo for the rest of my life. I can no look at what needs to be done and think I can perform some tasks when I am better. Time management totally changes when one has cancer. Before cancer, the extra reserve always seemed to be there. After cancer, it isn't.

In my humble opinion, the United States puts way too much emphasis on how much we get done in a day. Pick up any newspaper, look at any article online, or peruse any women's magazine and see how many times "saving time" in a busy world is mentioned.

Save for what? Many other cultures (and a few in the US) feel that spending time with family and friends is more important than anything else, including work. What a novel thought!

I no longer try to see how much I can get done in a day. Some days all I can do is take care of myself. In other words, do nothing but eat and sleep. There is no reserve in the tank. I try not to plan too much in one day for that same reason. I may be in bed for the next several days if I overdo.

Someone once told me that the body is like an oil lamp. If we shine our light and try to take care of everyone else without pausing, we burn out. We need to stop occasionally and replenish the oil. If we do this, our light can continue to shine and inspire others.

I constantly have to remind myself that if I don't feel good, I am no use to anyone else. If I am too busy, I have no time for friends and family.

So, renew your oil. Chill for a day or two. Instead of fighting the fatigue, make it a "jammie" day. Wear your pj's all day and relax! You are not wasting time; you're making it so you can do more in the long run. The world got along without you before you were born, and it will be okay now!

Reorganize your thinking, figure out your priorities, and replenish your oil. You will be healthier and happier for it. Meanwhile, your light shines so you can help others get through the darkness! And this is really what life is all about.

INSIGHT 17

Step-by-Step to Chemo

Step-by-step, I enter the hospital where the treatment center for my cancer is located. I left my car with the parking valet and placed the token in my purse. I walk up a flight of stairs. Step-by-step I walk down a long hallway. I pass a snack shop with delicious coffee and a beautiful gift shop.

I pass the elevators that take me up to the second floor, where I have my twice-yearly bone marrow biopsies. These are necessary to follow my progression with the cancer. The nurses there know me by name and are so kind to me. Nurses always are! Step-by-step, I continue and make a sharp turn. I could do this route in my sleep. Finally, I spot the huge sign that says, "Cancer Center" and the desk where I sign in.

I have been making this journey for many years now. I progressed from monthly appointments to see the oncologist and receive blood work to five times a month to receive shots each day.

Sometimes while making this walk, I just try to stay numb. Other times, my emotions overwhelm me. I remember the naivety of thinking nothing was wrong at first. I recall the doctor soberly telling me the average time to live with this cancer was eight years. I am close to hitting that benchmark and intend to keep going.

I think about all the changes the cancer has made in my life. I reflect negatively on the worst side effect from the chemo. I lost even more of my hearing and went from being hard of hearing to profoundly deaf. I miss so many conversations and sounds people take for granted now. I think about the constant fatigue, the muscle aches, the blistering skin for days afterward at the injection sites. I know I was fortunate to escape the hair loss and nausea so many people have.

My beautiful and loyal service dog has been faithfully by my side every single minute for a long time. But now at age thirteen, she has severe arthritis and is limping badly. I have made the difficult decision not to take her on that long walk. She has to stay home now. I miss her desperately and wonder if she recognizes the antiseptic smell of the hospital and chemo when I return to my apartment. She is terribly missed by many people, but I have to do what's best for her.

I wish desperately that I had a type of cancer where the treatments would end. That I could quit this long journey. That I could have the doctor tell me I only had to come back once a year—or never. While other patients have a goal and can mark off the number of treatments, those of us with blood cancers know we will be on chemo until it no longer works. Even better, I wish I had no cancer at all.

I do get depressed, and people ask me how I do it. My answer is that I am still alive and enjoying life. My wonderful oncologist switched around my treatments, so I was able to take a weeklong cruise recently to Alaska. I am still savoring that trip and looking at my pictures.

I mentally shake myself as soon as I sign in. I have entered another world now. All the staff there knows me by name. As I have my blood work done and chemo shots administered, I talk to the staff about their families. I chat happily with the people at the desk. I realize I have a whole new family that I love.

My oncologist always seems happy to see me, and I am thrilled to see her. We chat about her daughter in college, my travels, and my writing—just like good friends do. I feel like she is a best friend who is keeping me alive!

Yes, this is my new normal. It is never a journey I would have chosen. But it chose me. And as sad as I feel, as difficult as that journey step-by-step is, I am at peace. I have made new friends, found a caring medical community, and best of all, I am alive! That is how I do it!

INSIGHT 18

Can a Cancer Diagnosis Cause PTSD?

We all vividly remember receiving the diagnosis of cancer. We remember where we were, who was with us, and every detail of the room we were in. We remember parts of what the doctor told us, but most likely not everything. In my case, it was a cruel statement that the timeline for me to live was around 104 months. I shut down completely while she droned on about treatments. I thought, "My wonderful and happy life is changed forever."

Once a person is given the diagnosis of cancer and life-changing news, there is often a danger of developing post-traumatic stress disorder (PTSD). What do I mean by that? Isn't that for people like soldiers who have been in serious combat?

The diagnosis originated with soldiers returning from wars, but now mental health professionals have discovered it can occur after any traumatic event, ranging from a car accident, to rape, to the diagnosis of a potentially fatal disease.

I know because I had all the symptoms. There are three stages of PTSD: avoidance, hyper vigilance, and reexperiencing the event.

Immediately after my diagnosis, I didn't answer the phone or want to talk to anyone. I went to bed with the covers over my head. I live alone, which makes it easier to avoid everyone. Fortunately, family and friends persisted in contacting me and didn't allow me to continue this behavior.

Hyper vigilance is common with cancer survivors. Ironically, this is often what saves us, just like soldiers who remain vigilant in case the enemy is approaching. We are often the ones who discovered the lump, the change in a mole, or in my case, the fatigue and anemia. But now every ache, every attack of diarrhea, every change in our bodies makes us worry that the cancer is worse. It is a constant battle for us to find a balance between overreacting and letting the doctors know if something is really wrong. The tricky part about this is stress caused by the worrying we do can cause more physical problems, such as ulcers, stomach problems, headaches, and other reactions.

Unfortunately, eight years after my diagnosis, as I approach that benchmark mentioned by the doctor, I still remember her words and am concerned. Despite the fact that I immediately switched to a more positive oncologist who constantly encourages me, I constantly fight to keep from reexperiencing that nightmare in the original oncologist's office.

What does the cancer survivor do if there are symptoms of PTSD? If one is continuing to experience flashbacks and constant fear from hyper vigilance, seek a therapist who is trained in trauma. The therapy concentrates on changing the memory, which is housed in the limbic (emotional) side of the brain. It takes twenty milliseconds for our fast-thinking brains to process these memories. With hard work, the memory can be switched to the neocortex, the decision-making (logical) side of the brain. Interestingly enough, this decision-making takes five hundred milliseconds for the brain to process. Therefore, to switch over is truly progress!

Other treatments for PTSD are conventional methods that include proper diet, adequate sleep, exercise, and relaxation methods. One of the most effective treatments for PTSD is yoga. There is also a specific type of therapy technique called eye movement desensitization and reprocessing (EMDR). This can be very successful when administered by a trained therapist. Journaling also is beneficial for those with PTSD. More on this subject can be found by researching the works of Bessel van der Kolk. This dynamo is a recognized trauma expert and has written several book and articles on the subject.

Why can't a person just "get over trauma?" The brain is very complex, and researchers are discovering when a traumatic event occurs, there is a marked increase of the hormone cortisol in the adrenal glands. This hormone regulates many bodily functions, such as metabolism, sugar levels, and blood pressure. After the person experiences a traumatic event, the event is registered in the amygdale (emotional) part of the brain. The cortisol never returns to the original baseline without treatment. This means that cancer survivors are undergoing changes in their bodies due to cancer cells and chemo treatments and can experience additional medical assaults to their bodies if traumatized.

Do not let PTSD go untreated. Monitor it carefully and seek help. I personally prefer changing my own thoughts from "I have 104 months to live" to "I am going to beat all the odds!"

INSIGHT 19

Cancer and Chemo Effects That Nobody Discusses

It all started with my teeth—yes, my teeth. I suffer from bruxism, which is a grinding of the teeth. I also have temporomandibular joint syndrome (TMJ) because the hearing aids I've worn for decades have misshapen my jaw. I have bitten through more mouth guards than I can count.

When I had the first two root canals, I didn't panic because of the bruxism and TMJ. Then there was the time I had five root canals in one year. I know now this likely was a precursor to my cancer diagnosis. I suspected something was going on, but no one seemed to be able to tell me.

The fatigue set in, and I didn't know what to do. A few months later, I was diagnosed with Myelodysplastic syndrome, and the most prominent symptom is anemia. I was fortunate to have excellent doctors who caught this.

I do find that most doctors don't warn their patients about potential side effects from a disease. I suspect part of this is because every single patient is different. I wish, however, I had more warning. I was fortunate because I never vomited or suffered hair loss, which are the two most widely known side effects. However, I experienced raging and unpredictable diarrhea. I finally mentioned this to my oncologist, who gave me an excellent medication that has helped immensely.

During my monthly chemo week, I also take some additional medications to help with this annoying problem.

Then the hearing loss occurred. I was always afraid of losing the rest of my hearing, since I had been hard of hearing since birth. I have lost almost all of it and desperately hang on to little bit that is left. I work very closely with my audiologist and oncologist and have frequent audiograms to monitor the remaining hearing. They work together well, and I am very lucky.

More severe dental problems began to haunt me. I have had several teeth pulled, which is never fun. The dentist tells me I am unable to have implants because of the cancer. Also some of the cavities and decay are due to dry mouth, which is a side effect from the chemo.

I have a personal trainer at the YMCA. She is part of the Livestrong program and the one who told me that all chemo affects balance, no matter what kind. Why don't the doctors tell us this? More than once I have leaned over to pick something up and almost splattered on the floor! The solution is that the Livestrong program teaches cancer survivors wonderful exercises that help improve balance.

Next in my negative side effects were terrible stomach pains keeping me awake at night. My sharp oncologist immediately referred me to a gastroenterologist. After an endoscopy, I was diagnosed with esophagitis with multiple ulcerations. It actually sounds worse than it is, and medication helped this tremendously. When I looked it up on the internet, chemo was listed as one of the potential causes.

Another complaint in my litany of side effects is terrible muscle aches, like a charley horse in my legs. I got online and read this was one of the side effects from VIDAZA, my chemo drug. I asked my oncologist, who confirmed this, and she suggested OTC salve, which helps.

I had never been a victim of insomnia and felt sorry for people who were. I used to fall asleep as soon as my head hit the pillow. Then I started getting terrible bouts of it and even asked my oncologist for a prescription to help me sleep, blaming it on some life events, until I read something on Facebook that triggered an alarm. Yep—I looked up the potential side effects of VIDAZA, and insomnia is one of them!

Presently, I am feeling some neuropathy in my finger. The oncologist and I are not sure if this is a side effect since it is not listed, but she has recommended I take vitamin B.

I have always been a patient who waits until something is really wrong to go to a doctor, but I cannot afford to do that now. It is extremely difficult to find that healthy balance between being alert to any problems and obsessing over every single change in my body.

What is the answer? Fortunately, I have a wonderful oncologist who listens to me. I know that now is not the time to be afraid of overreacting. I discuss the changes with her, and each time she has listened and either said she will research it or referred me to a specialist. Every cancer survivor needs this type of relationship with their doctor. And patients need to do their own research using trusted websites or books.

Meanwhile, I am so thankful for the American Cancer Society, the National Cancer Institute, the organization Cure Today, and wonderful medical centers like the Cleveland Clinic, Mayo Clinic, MD Anderson, and many others that support research. I truly believe that most of us are experiencing more than the classic symptoms of nausea and hair loss. I suspect many people are experiencing muscle aches, dental problems, and the other symptoms, but they are not reporting it. We need to advocate for more research on the side effects of chemo, and we need to report them when we experience them. Many of us are living longer, which is wonderful. However, we need to receive more information so we can live happier and healthier lives. Only by speaking up can this be done.

INSIGHT 20

So You Have Cancer—Eat a Donut!

I must admit that I am one of those terrible people who never took care of my body very well when I was young. I worked long hours on responsible jobs. I pulled all-nighters to get my dissertation done. I ate way too much fast food and didn't start exercising on a regular basis until I was in my forties. Breakfast for me was coffee and a donut at the nearest bakery.

I didn't get enough sleep and felt guilty for taking time off when sick. I felt that relaxing and watching television was a complete waste of time. I stressed myself out, and I worried about everything, especially what people thought of me.

With age came some wisdom. I strove to be healthier. I tried not to worry as much. I began to eat less red meat and more veggies. I joined a local gym to exercise. I no longer worked two jobs and went to school, so I was getting more sleep. I received a beautiful service dog, who forced me to take healthy and wonderful walks.

However, I admit I still loved my donuts. My diet was better, but it still didn't contain enough healthy fruits and other good foods. I did not know how to read the labels of grocery products. I drank too much coffee.

Then, at age fifty-nine, I was diagnosed with a cancer. My whole attitude toward my body changed. I realized the truth of the biblical affirmation that "the body is the temple."

Fortunately, my wonderful oncologist told me nothing I did caused this cancer. I am so thankful for her, because I would have done the blame game and beat myself up. All the research I have read confirmed that with this type of cancer, one little itty bitty cell went haywire. I did not need to feel guilty on top of the other stresses of dealing with cancer.

I did reform. My refrigerator now has fruits and veggies. I joined the Livestrong program at my local YMCA. In addition to exercising regularly, I pay out of pocket for a personal trainer once a week. She does marvelous things to help me with my balance and has become a wonderful friend.

I also joined the free nutrition classes at the Y, and boy, did I have a lot to learn! I had no idea how much reading labels and careful monitoring of foods is necessary. The salt and sugar in packaged and canned foods just shocks me. The nutrition program at my YMCA is fantastic. Not only do we have a great nutritionist, but monthly we go to a local grocery store with another nutritionist who is a cancer survivor. She brings samples for us to eat, so we can find food we both like and is healthy.

However, I did not change everything. I still eat out frequently because I am single and eat better with friends. I am careful about what I order, and dessert is not even an option.

But I still love my donuts! The dietician and I have an ongoing friendly argument. She tells me there is absolutely not one ounce of nutritional value in a donut—none, zero, and nada. I have pleaded my case. Isn't there dairy in the cream? I mention to her tongue-in-cheek about the protein in the nuts. I told her one time that she was making me feel guilty with every bite I ate, and she said she had done her job!

See, I blame the whole thing on the American Association of Retired Persons (AARP). A member used to get a free donut when one orders a large coffee at Dunkin' Donuts. They do not do it anymore probably due to people like me!

We have laughed and joked about it, but we do agree. Everyone needs to slip something unhealthy into their diet once in a while. Every morning, breakfast is a hardboiled egg and toast. However, once a week I go and get my donut. I savor it, I enjoy it, and I love it!

And you know what? Gee whiz, I have cancer! We all know subliminally we are going to pass away sometime. Cancer just forces us to face that reality sooner.

Call it rationalization. But when I am on my deathbed, am I going to regret having a donut once a week? Or will I regret that I did not seize the day and spend more time with my loved ones? I think we all know the answer to that question.

So do not take yourself so seriously. Carpe diem—seize the day! Enjoy life and have that donut! It may not be healthy for your body, but it sure does help your spirit! And that is what counts.

INSIGHT 21

I Am More Than My Cancer

I love to write, and the writing I do is therapeutic for me. I enjoy using my talent with words to help encourage others.

However, I am afraid that people think I am obsessed with cancer since I write so much about it. Like most cancer survivors, nothing could be further from the truth.

Naturally, the shadow of cancer is always hanging over us, whether we are worried about a worsening cancer, going in and out of remission, or hoping for a new miracle drug to appear. The cancer is always in the back of my mind, sort of like a little gnat swarming around my brain. Sometimes that gnat lands on me, especially the five days I go in for chemo every month. However, I simply do not have time to be watching that gnat otherwise. Every one of us has a life to live with our families, our friends, our jobs, and our lifestyles. We are all different, like a kaleidoscope, constantly turning and changing. Diversity is what makes life interesting.

Each of you is more than the cancer you have and know what your loves and interests are. Let me explain how I am more than a cancer survivor.

I have a service dog that is my soul mate, friend, ears, and fur baby. I have done programs all over the country with her. I have written a picture book and several articles about her. I was more upset when she injured herself recently than when I was out of remission. At least I understood what was happening, but she didn't. We have many friends, both human and canine, that we have met on our journey.

I am an avid reader and belong to a book club. We meet monthly, and I get together with other people who love books. It is a highlight of my social life, and I rarely miss it. I have many more books on Kindle than I can ever read, and admit I am an addict!

I am a huge sports fan, and presently I am in mourning because my baseball team was eliminated from the playoffs. I live in Lebron James country and follow basketball closely. I have been an Ohio State fan and attended games for over forty years. I don't think about chemo while watching all my sports.

I have been hard of hearing all my life and have presented at national conventions. I have written several articles and was part of a local support group for decades. I even taught a class called Deaf Culture at the college level.

I have a church that I love, and the congregation and minister mean the world to me.

I enjoy traveling and putting pictures from my trips into scrapbooks.

I am so fortunate to have a wonderful family, friends, neighbors, and people I cherish. I am a friend, sibling, cousin, neighbor, church member, reader, dog lover, and the list goes on and on.

Who are you? List all the fascinating parts of your kaleidoscope, and remember this during the hard times. Many of you have even more roles than I do in your fascinating lives, such as wife, mother, grandmother, great grandmother, and daughter. Cancer doesn't change who we are.

I am not obsessed with my cancer. I have to go to doctor visits, endure chemo monthly, and follow a less rigorous schedule than I used to. I also try to exercise and consume a better diet. I want to find time to encourage other cancer survivors on this crazy roller-coaster ride we are on, which was not of our choosing.

We battle cancer not to just obtain remission and live. We battle cancer so we can enjoy all the other parts of our complex lives.

Remember, you are not dying with cancer but living with it. Toss that worrisome gnat aside when you can. You are more than your disease. Know this and take advantage of every second you have!

INSIGHT 22

Even with Cancer, We All Need to Lighten Up!

One of the most interesting things I have learned on this roller-coaster ride with cancer is the importance of humor.

No, cancer is not funny. Neither are accidents, child and pet abuse, disease, and hurricanes. There are many disasters caused by nature and humans that happen on a daily basis. Unfortunately, we are bombarded by the news twenty-four seven reminding us about these horrible events.

If one follows the news about cancer, it can drive you crazy. I remember many years ago when I was a kid, a big scare occurred from a research study that "proved" red Jell-O caused cancer. Mothers across the country panicked and stopped feeding their kids red Jell-O. My own mother, who was always the epitome of calm, laughed. She felt a balanced diet was the key to anything and was not worried at all. Years later the researchers confessed the results of the study were skewed because they had given copious amounts of red Jell-O to tiny little mice, and human consumption of that much Jell-O comparatively was impossible.

When I was a counselor, I always said that stress makes any health problem worse. Have you ever picked at a hangnail, and the next thing you know it is bleeding? We know it is stupid, but we continue to do it. If we stress over a simple hangnail, imagine what we do to our bodies when we worry and fret and carry on. This is counterproductive.

I love to be around people who do not take themselves too seriously. I am on a patient advisory council at the hospital where I receive my chemo treatments. The first observation I made at our initial meeting of cancer survivors was the humor, the laughing, and the communal spirit we shared. Several of the members had undergone surgeries and pain I couldn't even fathom. I realized how lucky I was. But instead of obsessing, they made a big fuss over my service dog, talked about how to make the waiting room more bearable for other people, and were positive instead of negative.

I had a student who suffered from breast cancer and never missed a class during the rugged treatments. She joked with me that she did not need to shave as she wore a turban when her hair was gone. She not only survived, but went on to graduate and become an occupational therapist. What a fantastic attitude and an inspiring person!

Maybe this is one reason they are survivors. Every single one of us has a story. Life is a series of wonderful incidents. My dog makes me laugh every day rolling in the grass and loving life. My neighborhood children fill my heart with joy. I love to go out with friends and laugh and snicker. The cruises I have taken are better therapy for my cancer than any treatment. I believe that we should occasionally enjoy the piece of chocolate, dish of ice cream, or the donut.

Admit any mistakes you make. Regina Brett, in her book *God Is Always Hiring*, talks about the culture of Amish people, which is fascinating. The largest numbers of Old Order Amish in the world live near my home. They go back several centuries and do not drive cars, have electricity, or possess worldly things. They are also beautiful quilters. Each quilt made by an Amish woman has a tiny mistake on purpose. They are strict believers in the Bible and feel that the only perfect being is God. Therefore, they cannot make the perfect quilt. Think about that—not only admitting a mistake, but not allowing oneself to be perfect. I find that very refreshing!

So do not try to be perfect. It is all right to cry, to be in a grumpy mood, to not be the most wonderful patient all the time. Laugh at yourself. Everyone is still teasing me about going to my family doctor after receiving a panel of blood work. I was absolutely having a fit because my cholesterol was so high. I started telling him how I changed my diet and everything. He was rolling on the floor as he explained it was my good cholesterol—it was off the chart, and he guaranteed me I would never die of a heart attack. Sheepishly I calmed down, then laughed at myself and told all the cancer survivors in my nutrition class.

Lighten up, laugh at yourself, and don't try to be perfect, kiss your loved ones, and enjoy that dessert.

None of us get out alive anyway. But we can be serious and worry on our journey, or we can laugh and enjoy ourselves. It is our choice.

INSIGHT 23

What My Service Dog Has Taught Me about Accepting Life After Cancer

I honestly think the term "new normal" is overused, but I can't think of a better description. I don't know anyone whose life hasn't changed after cancer. Even the people who valiantly work and raise a family have to adjust their lives around chemo, doctors' visits, and medications. Some people have to quit their jobs and plow through the bewildering maze of paperwork to apply for disability. Other survivors, such as those with breast cancer, have to change their body image, which is extremely difficult.

I have made several drastic changes personally in my life. Some of these included moving to another town, changing careers, and going back to school for two advanced degrees. Each time I achieved a "new normal" and adjusted accordingly. However, the new normal for cancer has been decidedly different. I never sobbed as hard as when I was forced to retire from a job I loved because of the chemo.

I realize looking back that I cried because this decision had been forced upon me instead of making it voluntarily. The challenge for me was defining a purpose in my life after forty-two years of working many hours.

My new life went from planning all my activities around my working hours to enjoying myself and relaxing. This was a huge change, but not so bad once I did it! I would not want to join the workforce again, because I don't feel up to the challenges.

Parallel with the new lifestyle for me is the journey with my hearing ear dog, Sita. We have been partnered and spent every minute together for ten years. When I first received her at age three, we ran every day after work to a nearby school playground. She would roam the grounds, sniffing every foot of the place and chasing anything that moved, like a squirrel or a rabbit. She was in doggy heaven as witnessed by the joyous barking on the way to her favorite place. It is the only time she has ever barked, since service dogs are not supposed to. But she was so happy, I allowed it!

We later moved to another place directly on a golf course. As she aged and I became weakened by chemo treatments, we would settle for a walk around the driveways where the townhouses and apartments were located. There is a park in the middle of the complex. Between the park and the golf course, she could sniff to her heart's content.

Then she hurt her leg and began limping. We changed our normal again to staying outside at a picnic table in the park where she could lie down and enjoy the fresh air. Finally, that walk got too far, and now she is content to lie down on the grass directly in front of my apartment. Here she can be the queen diva and be petted by all the neighbors walking by. As the injury has progressed, she is only allowed outside on a leash. I was depressed and upset, while she was content to lie in the grass and sniff for hours.

If only I could be more like my dog. I have fought my new normal every step of the way. I have questioned every decision from quitting my job to forcing myself to relax. I still push too hard, and after holidays and special events, I am sleeping for days to recuperate. If the truth is told, some of this is due to simple aging. My friends and relatives still tease me about the sputtering I did the first time a student called me elderly. But—I am! I have two choices here. I can resent the new normal; I can fight it and be bitter about it. Or I can look on the positive side. I am never worried Sunday evenings about going to work Monday mornings. I do not have a mountain of papers to grade in my living room. I can watch *Law and Order* all night long if I wish and take naps in the afternoon!

I look at my dog and wonder if she ever dreams about her younger days running across the fields. She probably does as evidenced by her barking and moving her legs when she is dreaming, but she doesn't worry or fret. She sits outside, complacently sniffing the air, accepting belly rubs from the neighbors, and nibbling on her kibble like it is a piece of steak. We can fight our new normal or accept it. It took a dog to teach me which is better.

INSIGHT 24

Art Is Therapy for Cancer Survivors

I obviously love writing, but I hate doing artwork of any kind. Why, you may ask? It all goes back to my teachers in grade school. I had a young art teacher tell me I wasn't talented like my sibling, and I needed to color between the lines. On the other hand, I had an English teacher who told me I had a gift for writing. Enough said. I love writing!

It wasn't until I became older when I realized writing was therapeutic for me. After my mother died, then my upsetting cancer diagnosis, I immersed myself into my writing. Happier times also inspired me. When I received my gorgeous service dog, I wrote a picture book and several articles on her.

When I write, there is something to be said about putting my thoughts down on paper. Most writers type their articles and books on a computer. I write my first draft in longhand. The words flow freely from my brain to my hand to the paper and then to the computer screen. I know this is my art form.

I recognize that music is a wonderful art form for healing. With my limited hearing, I can't enjoy this as much as most people. However, when I travel alone, I turn the car radio on high, and an uplifting song never ceases to inspire me.

But anything with drawing, watercolor, or paint scares me to death. Therefore, I was hesitant when my personal trainer and friend at the Livestrong program at my local YMCA asked me to attend a new venture at the local art museum. I honestly did it as a favor to her. I explained I couldn't do art, period. She assured me the medium used would be easy, and I didn't need to be a great artist.

Reluctantly, I entered the classroom a few days later. First, we took a tour of the museum. The display being showcased was on football around the country. I was thrilled because I love sports. I happen to live where the Pro Football Hall of Fame is located, so this display was special. But I dreaded sitting down to do the art project and wanted to skip to the lunch part.

We did a project called alcohol art. No, it is not drinking wine while doing artwork, which I would have enjoyed! Rather it was pouring special inks on paper treated with rubbing alcohol.

Then the ink was used to create the illusion. We could dabble, blow on the ink, color around the edges, or do anything we wanted. The two art therapists, who were our leaders, were extremely encouraging.

I didn't get off to an auspicious beginning because I got more ink on my fingers than on the paper. I went over to the sink, groaning to myself. I knew this would be a mistake. I spent ten minutes trying to get the ink off my fingers. I didn't believe the therapists when they said the bright ink would eventually come off. I hoped this would get me out of the project, but they chose to ignore me.

I sullenly went back to my picture. I began to work on it, and the colors mesmerized me. I dabbled, blew on the paper, and watched the pictures form. I felt like a child again. This time I was not being forced to stay within the lines! The leaders gave me a second sheet of paper, and I started working on that one. They showed me how to do multimedia with my art and helped me cut and paste my results.

When we were finished, the results stunned me. The entire group had done wonderful work. The leader suggested that since my artwork was bright and colorful with lots of balloons, maybe I was signifying happiness. I looked at her in amazement because she was right. We talked among ourselves about some of the ordeals we had been through with the cancer and shared tears of understanding and pain. We were survivors.

We did eventually get lunch and were done in two hours. We were all asked if we felt this was a helpful session. We mentioned that this activity helped us forget our cancer for a while. This is an important step to healing.

The YMCA asked our permission to temporarily put the artwork on display. If they had asked me in the beginning, I would have been embarrassed and said no. However, I was proud of my two pieces and agreed. Some people even wanted to purchase the art! I told them to go ahead and put the money into the Livestrong program.

All art can be healing, whether it's music, drawing, writing, or something else. Go and partake in a new activity no matter what the medium, because you may be better at it than you think. I guarantee you will have fun along the way!

INSIGHT 25

My Cancer Family

One of the bonuses I never expected as a cancer survivor was to meet and find a whole new family. I am single, and most of my family is scattered all over the country. However, I am fortunate to be a part of several other families who are my support group. They are more than casual friends I go to dinner with. They are people I depend on to be there when I need them. I laugh, cry, socialize, and spend holidays with them. Because of my friends, I am never alone on a holiday.

Some of them are people I shared a career with. Others are college friends I lived with for years in the dormitory. I meet with friends in a book club every month, where I share my innate love of books and reading. I have deaf friends who have supported me through losing my hearing. My church family is incredible, and I never enter the building without feeling their prayers, support, and warm embrace.

I even have a support group with my dog friends. It was my veterinarian and her staff who took care of my dog after surgery; because I had steps at home and she could not be with me. I have other friends who bring food for me after chemo when I am too tired to cook or go out. It is my friends who have accompanied me to doctor appointments and helped me through good and bad times. I have neighbors who check on me and help me with groceries and packages when I am too weak to carry them.

I have another wonderful and precious support group I never expected. When I was first diagnosed with cancer, my oncologist was very cold and unemotional. Her nurse was even worse and obviously didn't care about the patients at all. I quickly switched to another oncologist who is warm and supportive. She is one of those rare people who takes the journey along with every one of her patients. I asked her one time how she kept from burning out. Her answer was incredible as she explained that she has a higher power who gives her that strength and caring. I couldn't be on this difficult cancer journey without her and would have given up a long time ago. Her staff is all special too. The people at the front desk are always encouraging and friendly to the barrage of patients they see daily. Her nurses follow me every day of my chemo for five days straight and help me if I do not feel well. They are anxious after each one of my bone marrows to see whether the cancer is in remission.

The vena puncture people are always gentle and know me by name. The other patients in the waiting room have stories they want to share. The head nurse is a warm and caring person and always takes the time to stop and say hello. I often joke with her that I have never seen her sit down!

I am on a patient advisory council for the hospital where I am receiving treatment. I have met with the bravest and most inspirational people in the world. These wonderful volunteers have fought cancer for years and still use their precious time and energy to be on the committee. The hospital is in the middle of planning an exciting new cancer center and truly wants the input of the patients. Through this committee, I have met several people from the administration. I am impressed by all the time and effort they put into giving patients the very best of care. They are there from early morning to late at night.

I belong to a local YMCA that sponsors the Livestrong program. I have met some fabulous people there, including my trainer, who works with people recovering from chemo and has become a good friend. The two nutritionists are also special and have taught me a lot about reading food labels and making better food choices. As a result of this type of care, I try to reach out and encourage others who have cancer. I enjoy meeting with other survivors in the group and hearing their stories too. We support one another through good times and bad.

Through my writing, I have met even more cancer survivors and have become Facebook friends with courageous survivors all over the country.

I felt so alone when I found out I have cancer. I am convinced that the people who work with cancer survivors feel it is not a job, but a calling. They tell me constantly that I am family to them, and family helps one another through good times and bad. Otherwise, how could I get through this?

INSIGHT 26

With Cancer There Is Always Hope

One of my favorite books is *Man's Search for Meaning* by Viktor Frankl. It's a heart-wrenching story about a psychiatrist who was imprisoned in four terrible Nazi camps during the war. He used his time there to observe the other prisoners, and what he found surprised him.

As the world knows, over six million Jews died in concentration camps. Many of them did not die from being gassed and shot, but from disease, starvation, and the filthy conditions of the camps.

What intrigued Frankl was the fact the survivors were not always the fittest or strongest. He realized the people who survived had one thing in common. Each survivor he talked to had some kind of purpose in life and a reason to live. The purpose was different for each prisoner. It may have been a living relative, a home to return to, or a career that the person loved. Frankl's own purpose was clear to him. He decided to write a book when the war was over. He came close to giving up when the Nazis stole his notes. He wrestled with how he could go on until he realized the Nazis could not take away his mind. He had the book in his head. Frankl wrote the book in nine days after he was released from the camps!

A quote that Frankl uses in his book is from the famous philosopher Nietzsche. "He who has a why to live for can bear with almost any how."

Think about this. Hope and a reason for being were the sole factors in people surviving the worse torture, starvation, and humiliation the Nazis could inflict. Translate this to a cancer survivor. Hope is the one emotion we can control when a cancer is terminal. There is always hope for a new clinical trial, a new chemo, or a new immune-system booster. And if one is really ill and ready to let go, hope remains for relief in the next unknown step.

It is hope and the "why" that keeps us going. More than any medicine, radiation, or chemo, one thing is even more important. A reason for being, for staying alive, for loving life, can be miraculous. This love can be for a family member, a close friend, a pet, or a cause.

In my depressive moods, which hit with a vengeance, the ray of hope to get me through is usually a small but important gesture. A phone call from a friend, a card from a family member, my dog putting her face in my lap, or my cat crawling into bed with me all make me feel good. Grab this gesture, seize the day, and never give up hope. Try to do the same for others. If one has the why, the how will happen. Never forget that.

REFERENCES

American Cancer Society, Chemo Brain. www.cancer.org/expertvoices/2012/04/09/
    chemo-brain-it-is-real.

van der Kolk, Bessel. *The Body Keeps the Score: Brain, Mind, and Body in the Healing of Trauma*.
    New York: Penguin Books, 2014.
    www.goodreads.com/book/show/18693771-the-body-keeps-the-score.

Brett, Regina. *God Is Always Hiring: 50 Lessons for Finding Fulfilling Work*. New York: Grand
    Central Publishing, 2015.

Frankl, Viktor E. *Man's Search for Meaning*. Boston: Beacon Press, 1992.

Livestrong at the YMCA
https://www.livestrong.org/what-we-do/program/livestrong-at-the-ymca.

Niebuhr, Reinhold. The Serenity Prayer.
https://en.wikipedia.org/wiki/Serenity_Prayer.

Nietzsche, Friedrich.
http://www.goodreads.com/quotes/119387-if-you-know-the-why-you.

OTOTOXIC MEDICATION RESOURCES

Bauman, NG. *Ototoxic Drugs Exposed: The Shocking Truth about Prescription Drugs, Medications, Chemicals and Herbals That Can (and Do) Damage Our Ears.* Stewartstown: Integrity First Publications, 2010.

Biehl, J. "Ototoxic Medications: Is it Better to be Deaf Than Dead?" *Hearing Loss Magazine.* July/August 2017. 26-29.

Hammond, M. "RX Poison to the Ears: Making Sense of Ototoxicity." *Hearing Loss Magazine.* March/April 2013. 19-21

Kaufman, O. "Ototoxic Medications: Drugs That Can Cause Hearing Loss and Tinnitus." *League for the Hard of Hearing.* New York, 2000.

National Institute on Deafness and Other Communication Disorders (NIDCD). "Noise Induced Hearing Loss." May 15, 2015. http://www.nidcd.nih.gov/health/noise-induced-hearing-loss.

Rosen, M. "Drugs That Harm Your Hearing." *AARP.* October 8, 2014.
http://www.aarp.org/health/conditions-treatments/info-2014/drugs-that-harm-your-hearing.html?cmp=BAC-BRD-MC-HEARINGRC-N339.I006845TABOOLA.

Suss, E. *When the Hearing Gets Hard: Winning the Battle against Hearing Impairment.* New York: Plenum Press, 1993.

NATURAL TREATMENT RESOURCES

Aromatherapy: a review of MD Anderson Cancer Center recommendations
https://www.youtube.com/watch?v=3-WdBoLICbk.

Best Reiki books for free:
https://www.pdfdrive.net/reiki-books.html.

Essential Oils for Beginner
Am-books.com/2016/essential-oils-beginners-pdf.

Beginner's tips for using essential oils:
https://www.alesstoxiclife.com/beginners-tips-for-using-essential-oils.

Kefir benefits:
www.kefir.net/kefir-benefits.

ADDITIONAL RESOURCES

American Association for Cancer Research
http://www.aacr.org/Pages/Home.aspx (publishes magazine *Cancer Today*).

American Cancer Society and National Cancer Institute
https://www.cancer.gov (publishes magazine *Coping with Cancer*).

Aplastic Anemia and MDS International Foundation
https://www.aamds.org.

Cancer Care
Site for counseling support groups education and financial and copayment assistance.
https://www.cancercare.org.

Cure Today
www.http://Curetoday.com (publishes magazine *Cure*).

List of websites for information and support:
https://www.bestcancersites.com.

AFTERWORD

I realize that some people may want more detailed medical information than I have provided in this book. I intended it for the layperson, but I have added some additional medical terminology for the people who are familiar with these technical terms.

The name of my immune deficiency has a more recent term of IgA immune insufficiency.

The exact type of MDS I have is deletion 5Q subtype (del 5Q) of Myelodysplastic syndrome. The abnormal cells in my bone marrow are in this particular part of the marrow.

The PROCRIT shots I received when first diagnosed with anemia due to a low white blood count (leukocyte) was alfa epoetin.

The generic term for the REVLIMID I was on for seven years is lenalidomide.

The generic term for the VIDAZA I am presently on for treatment is azacitidine.

Technically these drugs are not all chemo drugs, but since this is the popular term that most people know, I have referred to these treatments as chemo throughout the book.

For more information, please contact https://www.aamds.org.

In February 2018 my stomach became infected and I am no longer on the VIDAZA shots. I have returned to the REVLIMID until my next bone marrow in August of 2018. Meanwhile, my oncologist is exploring other options for chemo including I.V. procedures. I feel very fortunate that there are constantly new medications and clinical trials out there to keep me living longer! It is a great time to be alive!

Printed in the United States
By Bookmasters